TEN THOUSAND
POISONOUS PLANTS
IN THE WORLD

PAUL ROCKETT

Perspectives is published by Raintree, Chicago, Illinois, www.capstonepub.com

Library of Congress Cataloging-in-Publication Data
Rockett, Paul, author.
  Ten thousand poisonous plants in the world / Paul Rockett
      pages cm.—(The big countdown)
  Includes bibliographical references and index.
  ISBN 978-1-4109-6878-4 (library binding)
  ISBN 978-1-4109-6885-2 (paperback)
  ISBN 978-1-4109-6899-9 (ebook PDF)
1. Poisonous plants.
I. Title. II. Series: Big countdown.

QK100.A1R63 2015
581.6'59—dc23   2014025520

Author: Paul Rockett
Illustrator: Mark Ruffle

Originally published in 2014 by Franklin Watts. Copyright © Franklin Watts 2014. Franklin Watts is a division of Hachette Children's Books, a Hachette UK company. www.hachette.co.uk

Printed in China.

Throughout the book you are given data relating to various pieces of information covering the topic. The numbers will most likely be an estimation based on research made over a period of time and in a particular area. Some other research may reach a different set of data, and all these figures may change with time as new research and information is gathered. The numbers provided within this book are believed to be correct at the time of printing.

CONTENTS

COUNTING DOWN THE PLANT KINGDOM

Plants can be found all over the world.

They are living organisms that, unlike animals, cannot move by themselves.

PLANTS WERE THE FIRST LIVING ORGANISMS ON EARTH

More than **2,000,000,000 years ago**, a form of algae started life underwater. Around **473,000,000 years ago** liverworts started growing on land. These evolved into many different plant forms. The last form, flowering plants, appeared **140,000,000 years ago**.

Plants produce their own food. They absorb energy from the sun, which along with carbon dioxide and water, enables them to make food and oxygen. This process is called photosynthesis.

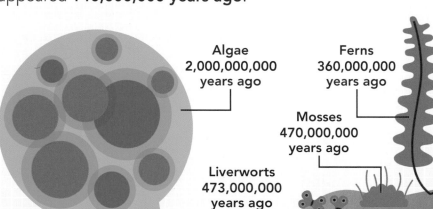

Algae
2,000,000,000
years ago

Ferns
360,000,000
years ago

Mosses
470,000,000
years ago

Liverworts
473,000,000
years ago

Conifers
290,000,000
years ago

Flowering
plants
140,000,000
years ago

Plants provide the world with oxygen, which is key to the survival of all animals. From plants, we also get food, wood and medicines.

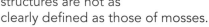

IF THERE WERE NO PLANTS YOU WOULDN'T BE ABLE TO LIVE.

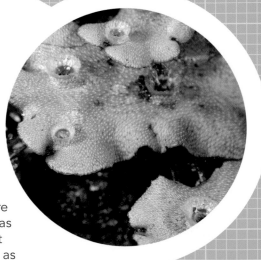

Liverworts are often put into the same plant group as mosses. However, there are differences, such as their leaf and root structures are not as clearly defined as those of mosses.

BOTANY

Botany is the scientific study of plants. A botanist is a plant explorer who studies plant structures and how they grow. They may do this in a science lab, or outside in the plant's environment, such as the rain forest or garden.

Numbers play an important role in botany. They are used for calculating statistics and looking for patterns within cell structures and rates of growth.

COUNTING THE RINGS OF A TREE

You can work out the age of a fallen tree by counting the rings on its stump. Each ring represents one year of growth. A large distance between each ring tells us that it was a wet and rainy year. A small distance between the rings tells us it was a hot year.

This tree was 14 years old.
- First year growth
- Rainy year
- Dry year
- Scar from forest fire
- 14th year of growth
- Bark

COUNTING PLANTS WITHIN A YARD

If you wanted to get an estimate of the amount and kind of plant life that grows in an area, make a square yard from cardboard and toss it into your yard or a nearby park. Wherever it lands, count and record the plants that you find.

A YARD OR PARK

A square yard is a good size—it shouldn't take too long to count all of the life that you capture within it.

You can then multiply this amount by the size of the yard or park. This will give you an estimate of the number of plants and plant species within the entire yard or park.

THERE ARE 321,212 SPECIES OF PLANTS

Plants grow all around us, in gardens and parks, but also in less accessible places, such as rain forests, deserts, and at the bottom of the ocean.

The large number of plant species all over the world makes the task of counting and identifying each one impossible. However, many people attempt to do this, with differing results. The number of plant species identified varies from **300,000** to **380,000**.

The World Conservation Unit estimates the number of plant species as being **321,212**. They have divided plant life into five categories: flowering, conifers, ferns, mosses and liverworts, and red and green algae.

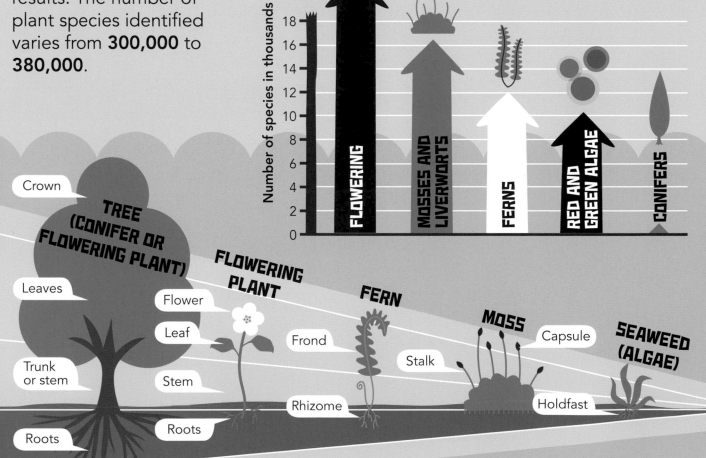

Number of species in thousands

300
250
18
16
14
12
10
8
6
4
2
0

FLOWERING

MOSSES AND LIVERWORTS

FERNS

RED AND GREEN ALGAE

CONIFERS

TREE (CONIFER OR FLOWERING PLANT)
- Crown
- Leaves
- Trunk or stem
- Roots

FLOWERING PLANT
- Flower
- Leaf
- Stem
- Roots

FERN
- Frond
- Stalk
- Rhizome

MOSS
- Capsule

SEAWEED (ALGAE)
- Holdfast

PARTS OF A PLANT
Most plants have roots, leaves, and stems. Plants may have parts that differ from each other, but they all have elements that help them perform similar functions. For example, the frond of the fern is similar to the leaf of a tree, and the capsule on moss is similar to a flower.

ROOTS

Roots keep plants firmly connected to the ground. In flowering and coniferous plants, there are two main kinds of roots:

Fibrous roots ••••••••••
These are spread out in many directions and all tend to be the same size.

•• **Taproots**
This is one large root with smaller roots coming off it. Root vegetables, such as carrots and parsnips, are taproots.

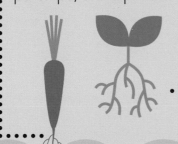

IDENTIFYING PLANTS

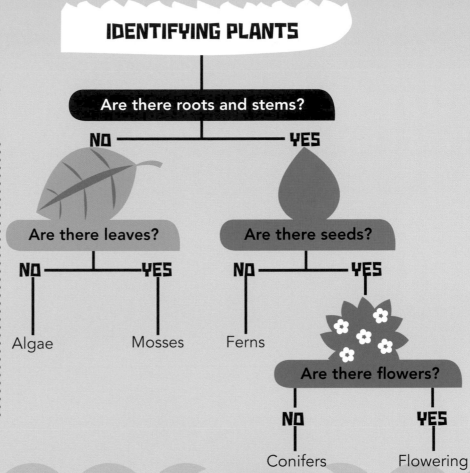

Are there roots and stems?

NO — YES

Are there leaves?

NO — YES

Algae   Mosses

Are there seeds?

NO — YES

Ferns

Are there flowers?

NO — YES

Conifers   Flowering

ALGAE

Not all scientists include algae as a type of plant. Algae do not always appear with a rootlike structure. In fact some, like the microscopic diatom, exist as just a single, individual cell.

DIATOM

Algae are largely found in areas of water, on the surface or bottom of lakes, rivers, and oceans. Some types of seaweed and kelp are forms of algae. Many scientists believe that the blue-green algae were the first living things to appear on Earth.

SEAWEED

FUNGI

Fungi are organisms that include mushrooms, yeasts, and molds. They used to be part of the plant kingdom, but since 1969 they have been separated into their own kingdom. They may look like plants, but they have a different cell structure and don't produce their own food. In fact, many scientists believe that fungi are more closely related to animals than to plants.

64,242 PLANTS ESTIMATED AT RISK OF EXTINCTION

Some scientists have estimated that one in five species of plant is at risk of dying out. If there are 321,212 species of plant, that's 64,242 plants at risk.

THREATS TO PLANT LIFE

The main threat to plant life is caused by humans, largely through the clearance of natural habitats for agriculture and industrial development.

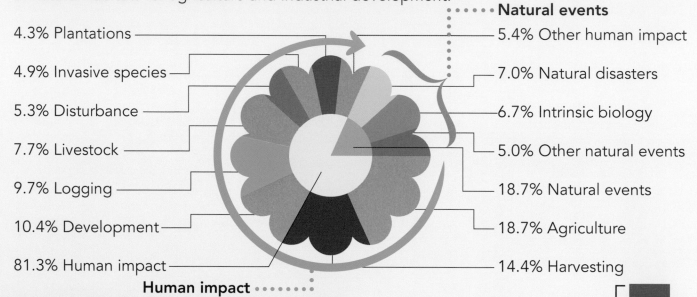

Natural events

4.3% Plantations

4.9% Invasive species

5.3% Disturbance

7.7% Livestock

9.7% Logging

10.4% Development

81.3% Human impact

Human impact

5.4% Other human impact

7.0% Natural disasters

6.7% Intrinsic biology

5.0% Other natural events

18.7% Natural events

18.7% Agriculture

14.4% Harvesting

FROM VULNERABLE TO EXTINCT

The large number of plant species makes it very difficult for botanists to assess the actual number that are at risk of extinction. The International Union for the Conservation of Nature took a sample of **15,674 plant species** and found that **121** were extinct and **9,390** were threatened by extinction.

The plants were placed in the following categories:

Vulnerable: high risk of endangerment in the wild

Endangered: high risk of extinction in the wild

Critically endangered: extremely high risk of extinction in the wild

Extinct in the wild: known only to survive in botanic gardens

Extinct: no known examples remaining

Out of the **15,674 plants** assessed, just under **60%** were found to fall into the vulnerable to extinct categories. If we apply this percentage to the **321,212 species of plants** then it's possible that approximately **192,400 plants** are at risk. That's nearly **three out of five plant species** at risk!

RESULTS FROM SAMPLE SELECTION:

15,674 PLANT SPECIES

Vulnerable: 4,914

Endangered: 2,655

Critically endangered:1,821

Extinct: 121

VULNERABLE

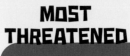

Name: Eastern Cape giant cycad
Plant category: Cycad, a species that links ferns and conifers
Habitat: coastal areas, river banks, and mountain foothills of South Africa
Threats: destruction for vacation resort developments and use in traditional medicines
Population number: Estimated at **10,000**. Thought to have declined by **30%** in the past **50 years**.

ENDANGERED

Name: Bentgrass
Plant category: Flowering
Habitat: rocky slopes and open patches of land on islands off the southern Atlantic Ocean
Threat: erosion of land and fires; introduction of alien plants in habitats preventing their growth
Population number: It is estimated that fewer than **250** exist in the wild.

CRITICALLY ENDANGERED

Name: Amazon lily
Plant category: Flowering
Habitat: Colombian rain forests
Threat: large-scale deforestation
Population number: Unknown. None have been recorded in the wild since 1853. Thought to be extinct.

CRITICALLY ENDANGERED

Name: Jellyfish tree
Plant category: Flowering
Habitat: granite slopes near the coast of islands in the Indian Ocean
Population number: Thought to be extinct in 1930 until six trees were found in 1970. Today, **50 trees** are known to exist.

EXTINCT

Name: Cry pansy
Plant category: Flowering
History: Originally from France, growing in areas around limestone, its habitat was largely destroyed through quarrying. Plant population was also drastically reduced as it became a popular flower for collectors. Last seen in 1927.

LIFE FORMS THREATENED BY EXTINCTION

MOST THREATENED

Amphibians

Coral

The world's plants are as threatened with extinction as mammals.

Plants and Mammals

Birds

LEAST THREATENED

THERE ARE TEN THOUSAND POISONOUS PLANTS IN THE WORLD

Plants are unable to run and hide from their predators, so some have developed other means of protecting themselves. Some plants, like rosebushes or cacti, have thorns or spines to discourage animals from coming near them. Other plants contain poison, which can make animals incredibly sick or even kill them.

There are around **10,000 poisonous plant species**. They can release their poison by touching or by eating them, some causing short-term illness, others death.

Poisonous plants have toxins that can be found in their sap, leaves, or berries.

MOST POISONOUS

Many botanists consider the castor oil plant to be the most poisonous plant in the world. The castor oil plant grows in tropical conditions and produces a highly toxic seed called the castor bean.

CASTOR BEANS

If you eat a castor bean that breaks open inside your digestive system, you may find that within:

2–3 HOURS — you experience a burning sensation in your mouth and throat, stomach pain, and diarrhea containing traces of blood;

1–3 DAYS — you experience severe dehydration and a decrease in urine;

3–5 DAYS — you die.

THE BELLADONNA PLANT can be found growing wild in Europe, North America, and Southwest Asia. Also known as deadly nightshade, all parts of this plant are poisonous.

Eating a single leaf will kill you.

Eating **five berries** will kill you.

1 2 3 4 5

Eating the roots will kill you.

STINGING NETTLES

The most common stinging plant found in Europe, North America, and parts of Asia is the stinging nettle.

Nettles have hairy leaves and hairs on their stems.

Each hair has a bulbous tip. Upon contact this tip breaks off to leave a sharp, needlelike tube that pierces the skin, injecting a toxin. This toxin can leave raised bumps on the skin and cause an itching sensation that can last up to **12 hours**.

GYMPIE-GYMPIE STINGING TREE

The gympie-gympie stinging tree, found in the rain forests of Australia and Indonesia, is the only stinging plant that is believed to cause death from its stings. It has been known to kill dogs and horses that have brushed up against it.

A gympie sting has been described as like being burnt with hot acid and electrocuted at the same time!

CARNIVOROUS PLANTS

All plants get their food through photosynthesis. However, some plants are themselves predators and will trap and eat animals in order to get more nutrients to help them grow.

PITCHER PLANTS

There are **120 species** of pitcher plants. The giant pitcher plant is the largest of all carnivorous plants. Discovered in the Philippines, it produces a sweet-smelling nectar inside its jarlike head.

Nectar attracts insects and small mammals that fall inside.

Creatures are unable to climb out due to the sticky walls inside and end up dissolving in a pool of acid and enzymes.

VENUS FLYTRAPS

The Venus flytrap eats small insects, enclosing them within its traps.

The trap opens at about a **45-degree angle**.

45°

20

The trap closes when an insect touches a single hair twice, or **two separate hairs** within **20 seconds** of each other.

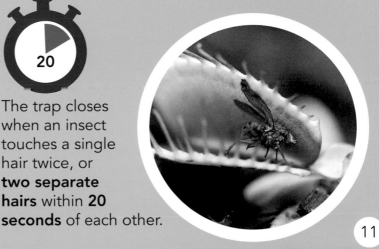

OXYGEN IS RENEWED BY PLANTS EVERY TWO THOUSAND YEARS

The food we eat and the oxygen we breathe are both formed by plants through a process called photosynthesis.

PHOTOSYNTHESIS INGREDIENTS

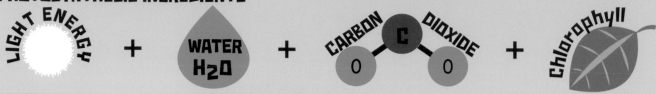

LIGHT ENERGY + WATER H_2O + CARBON DIOXIDE O C O + Chlorophyll

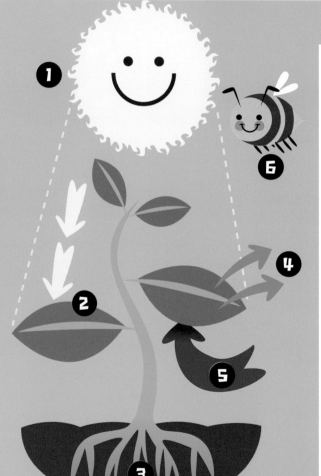

STEP 1
Light from the sun shines down onto a plant. The plant's cells absorb this light.

STEP 2
Inside the plant's cells is a substance called chlorophyll. Chlorophyll traps the sun's light.

STEP 3
Water is absorbed into the plant through its roots underground. Water is made up of the elements hydrogen and oxygen.

STEP 4
Inside the plant, the oxygen and hydrogen from the water separate from each other; the oxygen is released into the atmosphere.

STEP 5
Carbon dioxide from the air is absorbed through the plant's leaves. The carbon dioxide combines with the hydrogen to make a form of sugar that the plant can use as food.

STEP 6
Animals also use the sugar produced by the plants as food.

Oxygen = O_2
Carbon dioxide = CO_2
All plants release oxygen into Earth's atmosphere. All living creatures breathe in oxygen to keep them alive and breathe out carbon dioxide, which is absorbed by plants.

FOOD CHAINS

Plants are at the start of every food chain. All animal life depends upon plants for food.

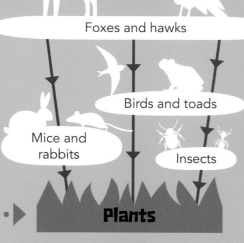

Foxes and hawks

Birds and toads

Mice and rabbits

Insects

Plants

CHLOROPHYLL COLOR

Chlorophyll is the reason why most plants are green. During photosynthesis plants absorb the different colors that make up the sun's light. However, chlorophyll is not able to absorb the color green, so it reflects it back, which is why we see green plants.

REFLECTED GREEN

LEAF

EARTH'S OXYGEN

Scientists believe that when Earth was formed **4,500,000,000 years ago**, its atmosphere was largely made up of carbon dioxide. The process of photosynthesis by plants meant that the proportion of oxygen increased. This increase in oxygen helped develop the variety of life that is now on Earth.

OXYGEN

70% comes from algae and small organisms in the oceans.........

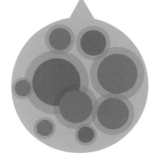

28% comes from tropical rain forests........

2% other ....

OXYGEN IN THE AIR IS RENEWED BY PLANTS EVERY 2,000 YEARS.

Each carbon dioxide molecule in the atmosphere is absorbed into a plant every **200 years**.

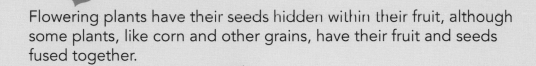

A POMEGRANATE CAN HAVE AS MANY AS 1,370 SEEDS

Flowering plants and conifers grow from seeds and create seeds.

Conifers have their seeds protected inside cones. A cone's scales open up to release its seeds.

Flowering plants have their seeds hidden within their fruit, although some plants, like corn and other grains, have their fruit and seeds fused together.

One apple can produce as many as **20 seeds**.

A pomegranate can contain as many as **1,370 seeds**.

Some orchids have seedpods that can hold around **3,000,000,000 seeds**.

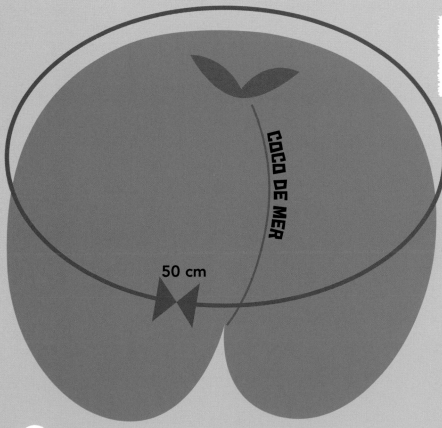

COCO DE MER

50 cm

A NUT IS A FRUIT MADE OF A HARD SHELL AND A SEED INSIDE.

Shell

HAZELNUT

Kernel

The largest seed in the world comes from the nut of a plant called coco de mer. The hard shell has two lobes giving it the name "the double coconut." It can measure up to **20 inches** (50 cm) in circumference and can weigh up to **39 pounds** (17.6 kg).

SEED DISPERSAL

Plants disperse their seeds in different ways so that when plants grow they don't crowd each other or have to compete for water or light.

WATER

Plants on a riverbank or seashore drop their seeds into the water. The seeds then float off to grow. Some coconuts have floated **1,243 miles** (2,000 km) before finding dry land.

EXPLOSIONS

Some plants have seedpods that explode, scattering their seeds. As a pod begins to dry out, it shrinks. At the same time, the seeds ripen and grow bigger, causing them to burst out of the pod.

ANIMALS

Some plants have seeds that are sticky or have small hooks that attach to animal fur. The animal then transports the seeds to a new place. Animals and birds also eliminate the seeds that are in the fruit they eat.

WIND

Some fruits are so light that they and their seeds can be blown away by the wind. The seeds of the dandelion flower get dispersed by the wind.

SPORES

Mosses and ferns do not have seeds. They produce spores. Spores are tiny reproductive cells. On ferns, they are often contained within tiny brown-black dots on the leaf. On mosses they can be found in their capsules. The spores are transported from the plants by wind or water. A single fern frond can hold up to **750,000 spores**.

The dandelion flower has bright yellow petals. When these petals die out, seeds grow on the flower head.

One dandelion flower head can produce **200 seeds.**

TRAVELING DISTANCE:

99.5% of dandelion seeds travel less than **33 feet** (10 m).

0.05% travel more than **33 feet** (10 m).

0.6 miles

0.014% travel more than **0.6 miles** (1km).

When a seed starts to grow, it begins a process called germination. This starts with a tiny root and a shoot sprouting out through the coating of the seed.

PARTS OF A SEED

........Shoot
........Seed coat
........Food store
........Root

Leaves

Plant

Seedling

Stem

GERMINATION

Seed

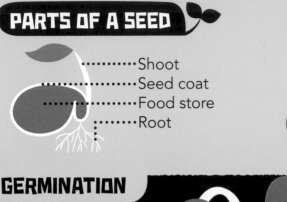

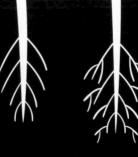

WHEN DO SEEDS GROW?

Seeds can survive for a long time before they begin to grow into a plant. The time it takes for a seed to germinate depends on it receiving enough water and being in the right type of soil at the correct temperature.

Number of days for a seed to germinate according to temperature

Degrees F°/C°	32°/0°	41°/5°	50°/10°	59°/15°	68°/20°	77°/25°	86°/30°	97°/36°
Parsnip	172	57	27	20	14	15	32	
Onion	136	50	13	7	5	4	4	13
Carrot		50	17	10	7	7	6	9
Pea		46	14	9	8	8	6	9
Tomato			43	14	14	6	6	9
Pepper			25	25	13	8	8	9
Watermelon			12		12	12	4	3

CAMPION

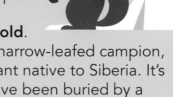

OLDEST SEED
The oldest seed to grow into a plant was dated as **32,000 years old**. It grew into a narrow-leafed campion, a flowering plant native to Siberia. It's believed to have been buried by a squirrel during the Ice Age.

RATES OF GROWTH

Once germinated, it can take an apple seed **six to ten years** to grow into a tree and bear fruit. However, it's very hard to grow an apple tree that will produce a large crop from seeds. Because of this, fruit-bearing apple trees are mainly grown from grafting, which can help them produce fruit more quickly. Grafting is a technique in which parts of two plants are joined together. To achieve this, the stem of one plant's rootstock needs to be cut and joined to the stem of another plant.

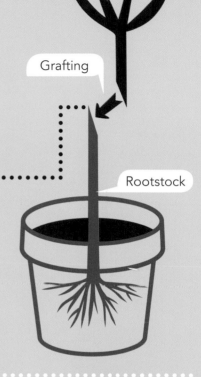

Grafting

Rootstock

Rootstock can determine a plant's eventual size. Apple tree rootstock is sold with a tag telling the buyer how big the tree will grow once it's grafted.

The sizes are:

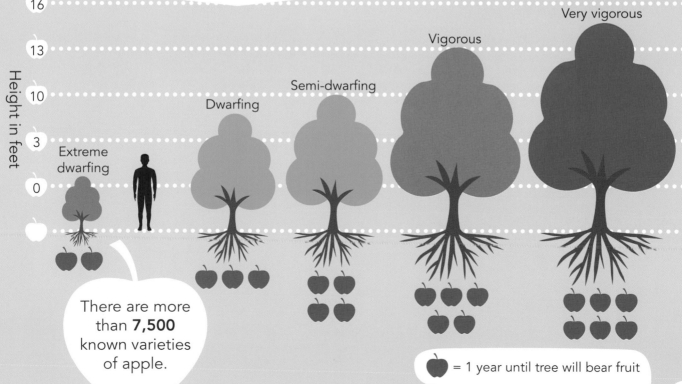

Height in feet

16
13
10
3
0

Extreme dwarfing

Dwarfing

Semi-dwarfing

Vigorous

Very vigorous

There are more than **7,500** known varieties of apple.

= 1 year until tree will bear fruit

THERE ARE MORE THAN 300 TYPES OF HONEY

Honey is made from nectar that bees collect from flowers. While collecting nectar, bees also collect pollen, taking part in the process of plant pollination.

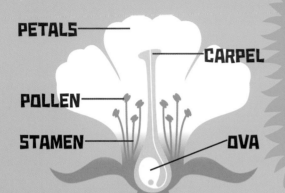

PETALS

CARPEL

POLLEN

STAMEN

OVA

Before flowers can produce fruit and seeds, they must be pollinated. This happens when the pollen from a flower joins to an ova hidden inside a flower.

Flowers contain stamens, at the top of which is the pollen. Flowers also have a carpel which holds an ova that the pollen needs to reach in order to allow the plant to grow its seeds and fruit.

POLLINATORS

Pollination is enabled by pollinators. They take the pollen from one flower to another. Pollinators include the wind, waves, human activity, and animals such as:

BEES   **BUTTERFLIES**   **BEETLES**   **ANTS**   **FLIES**   **BATS**   **HUMMINGBIRDS**

An estimated one out of every three bites of food comes to us through the work of animal pollinators.

ANIMAL POLLINATION

Many insects and birds feed off flowers. They are attracted to them by their bright colors and sweet smells.

Pollen is sticky and attaches itself to the creatures that have been drawn to the flower.

When the creature visits another of these flowers, the pollen gets rubbed from its body onto the top of the carpel.

Once the pollen has attached itself to the carpel, it travels down to join the ova. The plant has now been pollinated, and the pollen and ova join together to make seeds.

Some flowers are pollinated by the wind. Their pollen is carried through the air.

Hay Fever

Pollen contains proteins that can cause an allergic reaction in some people. This is known as hay fever.

Symptoms:

RUNNY NOSE

SNEEZING

ITCHY EYES

FLOWER POLLEN

Causes:

TREE POLLEN

GRASS POLLEN

BEES

It takes a colony of about **74,132 bees** to pollinate 2.5 acres (1 hectare) of fruit trees.

2.5 ACRES (1 HECTARE)

A worker bee gathers enough honey to make **1/10 teaspoon of honey** in its lifetime.

While collecting the pollen, bees feed off the nectar from flowers, which they carry back to their hives to make honey.

There are more than **300 different types of honey**. Each type is made from the nectar of a different flower.

THE TALLEST TREE IS 379 FEET (115.5 M) HIGH

Trees are the tallest free-standing living things in the world. They also live longer than any other organism on Earth.

The oldest tree is a jurupa oak tree in California. It is said to be **13,000 years old**, making it the oldest living organism on Earth. The oldest known person lived to be **123 years old**. If the life of the oldest tree were measured as being **24 hours**, then the oldest person would have been alive for **13 minutes and 36 seconds** of that time.

12 hours   12 hours   13 minutes and 36 seconds

Life span of oldest person

Life span of oldest tree

The broadest tree trunk is a Montezuma cypress, in Oaxaca, Mexico. The trunk's diameter is **46 feet** (14 m), with a circumference of **138 feet** (42 m).

The tallest living tree is a coast redwood growing in Redwood National Park in California. It measures **379 feet** (115.5 m) high.

The smallest tree is the dwarf willow tree. It rarely grows above **2 inches** (5 cm).

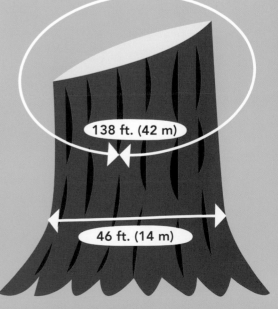

138 ft. (42 m)

46 ft. (14 m)

Tallest human ever: **8 ft. 11 in.** (2.72 m)

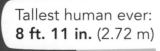

TREE, SHRUB, OR HERBACEOUS PLANT?

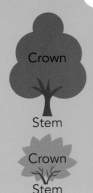

Crown

Stem

Crown

Stem

The difference between trees and shrubs is in the growth form of the stem. Trees have a single woody stem from which branches grow to form a crown. Shrubs have multiple woody stems that arise at ground level forming a crown at a lower level.

A herbaceous plant is a plant that does not have much wood and its stems are green and soft. You may hear people say that bananas grow on banana trees, but bananas actually grow on a herbaceous plant known as the musa.

DECIDUOUS TREES

Deciduous plants are those that lose all of their leaves for part of the year. Depending on the region, this usually coincides with winter. Leafless trees need less water. Before the tree sheds its leaves, the color of the leaves may change. This is because less green chlorophyll is made and other colors show through.

SUMMER   WINTER

An oak tree sheds around 250,000 leaves a year.

EVERGREEN TREES

An evergreen tree has leaves all year round and those leaves remain green. Most trees that have needles for leaves are evergreen. These leaves have been adapted to slow down the loss of water vapor, allowing them to survive in cold and dry seasons. They have a waxlike waterproof coating.

TREES HAVE LEAVES OF MANY DIFFERENT SHAPES AND SIZES

Simple   Doubly-serrated   Compound or lobed   Star-shaped   Heart-shaped or cordate   Lanceolate   Linear   Deltoid

100 SPECIES OF MOSS GROW IN THE ANTARCTIC

Few plants are able to grow in very dry or cold places, or where there isn't much sunlight.

Of the **16,236 species of moss** in the world, only **100** grow in the Antarctic. **Six different species** of moss grow on the islands of East Antarctica. The mosses that survive there have an unusual food source. In addition to the food they get from photosynthesis, they get extra nutrients from penguin poo left behind **thousands of years ago.**

- 1 year
- 2 years
- 3 years

The mosses on the islands of East Antarctica grow just **0.1 inches** (3 mm) a year.

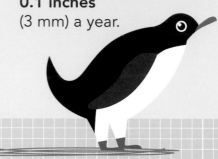

BIOMES

Earth is often divided up into different biomes. These are places that have specific temperatures and landscape that allow certain plants to grow there.

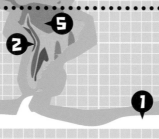

Equator

BIOMES:
- **Tundra:** treeless, cold climate
- **Taiga:** forested areas with wet summers and long, cold winters
- **Grasslands:** vast grassy terrain with hot summers and cold winters
- **Desert:** dry and hot with little plant growth
- **Tropical rain forest:** hot and wet densely forested regions
- **Temperate rain forest:** cool and wet forested regions
- **Polar:** very cold with permanent presence of ice and snow

ANTARCTICA ❶

Coldest place on Earth
Average temperature: −71°F/−57°C
Coldest recorded temperature: −128.6°F/−89.2°C
The majority of the Antarctic continent is covered by permanent ice and snow, leaving less than **1% of land** suitable for plants to grow. Due to the cold, harsh conditions on Antarctica, no trees are able to grow there, but some mosses have adapted to the harsh conditions.

ATACAMA DESERT, CHILE ❷

Driest place on Earth
Average temperature: 72°F/22°C

A cactus can grow in hot, dry places like deserts. Its roots are near the top of the ground so that it can take in water quickly when it rains. It stores water in its stem.

Only **three cacti** are native to this region. Because it rains very little there, these cacti get the majority of their water from the ocean fog that blows over the desert.

DASHT-E LUT, IRAN ❸

Hottest place on Earth
Highest recorded temperature: 158°F/70°C
No plants or creatures are known to live there.

SAHARA DESERT, AFRICA ❹

Average temperature: 86°F/30°C
Some plants in the Sahara Desert have extensive root systems that can go deep into the ground to get water. The roots of the *welwitschia mirabilis* go as deep as **164 feet** (50 m).

AMAZON RAIN FOREST, BRAZIL ❺

Average temperature: 81°F/27°C
The Amazon rain forest has a tropical climate, providing a constant supply of water and sunlight for broad-leafed plants.

40,000 different plant species can be found there. This is the largest variety of plant species to be found in one area.

SVALBARD, NORWAY ❻

Average temperature: 39°F/4°C
Only **165 species of plant** have been found to survive the tundra of Svalbard.

The Arctic buttercup lives there and is able to survive by living in groups close to the ground, which shelter them from the strong, cold winds.

UNDERWATER

Sea grasses found near the coastal waters of most continents are the only plants that can produce flowers under water. They are pollinated by the waves, which carry their pollen.

80–85 COCOA BEANS IN AN AVERAGE CHOCOLATE BAR

Plants provide a main source of food for all living creatures. Humans eat fruits and vegetables raw or cooked and also use them as ingredients in other foods, such as chocolate or bread.

THE WORLD'S LARGEST CUCUMBER MEASURED 3 FT., 7 IN. (1.1 M).

Fruit grows from the flower of a plant, but vegetables come from different parts of different plants.

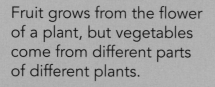

ROOTS: CARROTS

STEM: ASPARAGUS

LEAVES: CABBAGES

FLOWER: BROCCOLI

DIETS

Many animals just eat plants; they are called herbivores. Humans who eat only plants are called vegetarians or vegans.

It's important to have a balanced diet. This means eating a variety of foods to ensure that you receive the right nutrients your body needs to stay healthy. Some nutrients are easily found in meat and dairy products, but if you are a vegan, it's important that you eat the right foods to supplement your diet.

WHAT YOUR BODY NEEDS:	PROTEIN	CALCIUM	IRON	VITAMINS
Examples of food it can be found in:	Potatoes Beans and legumes	Broccoli Almonds Kale Dried apricots	Swiss chard Chickpeas Lentils Kidney beans	Carrots Oranges Bananas Spinach

BEANS AND LEGUMES

Beans and legumes are edible seeds from plants. They are often contained within protective pods and include lentils, black beans, chickpeas, lima beans, and kidney beans. Lentils have been found in the tombs of ancient Egyptians dating back to **2400 BC**.

COCOA BEANS COME FROM COCOA PODS, WHICH COME FROM THE CACAO TREE.

Over **3,900,000 tons** (3.5 million tonnes) **of cocoa beans** are produced annually and are transformed into products that contain cocoa. **80–85 cocoa beans** go into an average chocolate bar.

The cacao tree is an evergreen and is found in over **50 tropical countries**. It grows best within **15 degrees** north or south of the equator.

Cocoa beans are farmed in the following countries:
Ecuador·············
Brazil··············

Ivory Coast·········
Ghana··············
Nigeria············
Cameroon···········

Indonesia·····
Kenya
Tanzania

FROM CACAO TREE TO CHOCOLATE BAR

It takes **two to three years** after the cacao tree has been planted before it produces cocoa pods, its fruit.

Every year, cacao trees grow thousands of flowers. Only around **5%** of the flowers will produce a pod.

It takes around **five months** for each pod to ripen. Once they have been cut down, the beans are then removed from their pods. There are between **30–40 beans** inside a pod.

Next, the beans are dried, often in the sun. People rake them to help the moisture escape. This takes about **one week**.

The beans are fermented to bring out their flavor and prevent them from sprouting. This is done by wrapping heaps of beans in large leaves or placing layers of beans in wooden crates.

The chocolate liquor is blended with some cocoa butter and other ingredients, such as sugar and milk. It is mixed for hours and then poured into chocolate bar molds.

The individual bars are wrapped and delivered across the world for people to eat.

The dried beans are taken to a processing plant where they are cleaned and roasted.

The beans pass through rollers. This leaves chocolate liquor, cocoa powder, and cocoa butter.

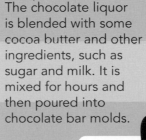
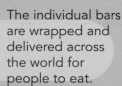

IT TAKES 14 TREES TO MAKE 2,240 LBS. (1 TONNE) OF MAGAZINE PAPER

Plants not only provide you with food but are used in items all around you, such as clothes and furniture.

Paper and cardboard are used as packaging for almost everything. Around **42%** of logging that takes place each year is for the production of paper.

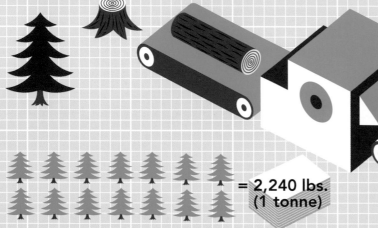

= 2,240 lbs. (1 tonne)

It takes **14 trees** to make **2,240 pounds** (1 tonne) of magazine paper. An average magazine weighs around **12 ounces** (340 g). There are **35,840 ounces** (1,016,047 g) in **2,240 pounds** (1 tonne). To find out how many magazines can be produced from **2,240 pounds** (1 tonne) of paper, divide **35,840 ounces** (1,016,047 g) by the weight of an average magazine.

2,240 pounds (1 tonne) of paper divided by the weight of one magazine = **2,987 magazines**.
It takes **14 trees** to make **2,987 magazines**.
It takes **1 tree** to make **213 magazines**. · =

213

COTTON

The majority of clothes worn in the world are made from cotton. Cotton grows as a soft fluffy ball that protects the seeds on cotton plants. Around **28 million tons** (25 million tonnes) **of cotton** are grown each year. Cotton was first used for clothing over **7,000 years ago**, in the Indus Valley, which is now part of India and Pakistan.

Plants are also used for dyeing clothes. This started over **5,000 years ago.** Plants that have been used for dye include:

Kamala tree = red
Pomegranate peel = yellow
Indigo fera plant = blue

MEDICINES

For hundreds of years, plants have been used as medicines. Today, many extracts from plants are still used to make medicines. **25%** of all medicines have been developed from tropical rain forest plants.

FOSSIL FUELS

Coal, gas, and oil are known as fossil fuels. They are formed from plants and small animals that died and decayed over **millions of years** and were covered by many layers of dirt under the ground. We use coal, gas, and oil as fuel. We burn these to keep us warm and to power cars and electricity. Oil is also used to make plastic.

OCEAN 300–400 MILLION YEARS AGO

Plants and animals died and were buried under layers of sand.

OCEAN 50–100 MILLION YEARS AGO

Sand and silt

Plant and animal remains

Over millions of years these remains were buried deeper, with heat and pressure turning them into fossil fuels, such as oil and gas.

TODAY

Sand and silt rock

Oil and gas

We drill down through layers of sand and rock to reach the fossil fuels.

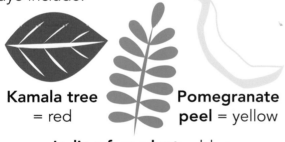

PLANT	USED FOR
Foxglove	Heart medication
Eucalyptus tree	Cough medicine
Quinine tree	Malaria prevention
Opium poppy	Pain reliever
Curare tree	Muscle relaxant

THE QUEEN OF THE NIGHT BLOOMS FOR ONE NIGHT EVERY YEAR

Among the huge number of plant life there are some unusual plants that can amaze and disgust.

CORPSE FLOWERS

DISGUSTING PLANTS

The *titan arum*, which is found in Indonesia, is one of the world's smelliest plants. It produces flowers about every six years, and when this happens, it smells like rotten meat. The flowering structure can reach over **10 feet** (3 m) in height. It is surrounded by a single leaf that can grow to **20 feet** (6 m) tall and **16 feet** (5 m) wide.

RAFFLESIA ARNOLDII

1 metre

The *rafflesia arnoldii* of Indonesia, is also sometimes called a "corpse flower" because it too smells of rotting meat. It has the largest flower of any plant in the world. Its flower has a diameter of around **3 feet** (1 m). The rafflesia is a parasite that lives off other plants.

TITAN ARUM

Height in feet

10.5

9

7.5

6

4.5

3

1.5

0

Titan arum is also known as the "corpse flower."

PARASITIC PLANTS

Plants that attach themselves to other plants and suck out nutrients from them are known as parasitic plants. These plants manage to insert roots into their host plant.

Mistletoe is a parasitic plant. Birds eat its seeds, which land on the host plant from bird droppings. Mistletoe can grow so large and bushy that it can be hard to spot the host plant's leaves among those of the mistletoe.

MISTLETOE ON AN APPLE TREE

GIANT WATER LILY

LARGE LEAVES

The giant water lily has a large circular leaf, also known as a lily pad, that can grow to over **8 feet** (2.5 m) in diameter. The leaf can support **100 pounds** (45 kg) of weight, as long as it is evenly distributed over the leaf's surface.

FOR ONE NIGHT ONLY

The night-blooming *cereus*, also known as the "queen of the night," is the name of a group of cacti that flower at night. Some of these only flower once a year. They grow in the deserts of Texas and northern Mexico. The flowers are trumpet-shaped and can grow to **4 inches** (10 cm) wide and **8 inches** (20 cm) long.

NIGHT-BLOOMING CEREUS

FURTHER INFORMATION

BOOKS

Project Science: Plants by Sally Hewitt (Franklin Watts, 2012)

Science F.A.Q.: Do Plants Really Eat Insects? by Thomas Canavan (Arcturus Pub., 2014)

Super Science: Flowering Plants by Rob Colson (Franklin Watts, 2010)

The World in Infographics: The Natural World by Jon Richards and Ed Simkins (Owlkids Books, 2013)

WEBSITES

Games and information on how to grow plants and information on the environmental issues surrounding tropical rain forests:

www.sciencekids.co.nz/plants.html

Activity with instructions on how to grow your own miniature garden:

kids.nationalgeographic.com/kids/activities/crafts/miniature-garden/

Fun games and quizzes plus information on the importance of rain forests:

http://therainforestrangers.com

Note to parents and teachers:

Every effort has been made by the publisher to ensure that these websites contain no inappropriate or offensive material. However, because of the nature of the Internet, it is impossible to guarantee that the content of these sites will not be altered. We strongly advise that Internet access is supervised by a responsible adult.

LARGE NUMBERS

1,000,000,000,000,000,000,000,000,000,000,000 = ONE DECILLION

1,000,000,000,000,000,000,000,000,000,000 = ONE NONILLION

1,000,000,000,000,000,000,000,000,000 = ONE OCTILLION

1,000,000,000,000,000,000,000,000 = ONE SEPTILLION

1,000,000,000,000,000,000,000 = ONE SEXTILLION

1,000,000,000,000,000,000 = ONE QUINTILLION

1,000,000,000,000,000 = ONE QUADRILLION

1,000,000,000,000 = ONE TRILLION

1,000,000,000 = ONE BILLION

1,000,000 = ONE MILLION

1,000 = ONE THOUSAND

100 = ONE HUNDRED

10 = TEN

1 = ONE

GLOSSARY

algae	a simple form of plant often found in water. Some seaweeds are algae.
allergic reaction	when your body reacts to a particular substance, causing irritation, such as itchy eyes or a rash
biomes	large areas on Earth that are defined by their plant life and climate
botany	the scientific study of plants
carbon dioxide	a gas that humans breathe out and plants absorb
carnivorous	the description of an organism that eats animals
chlorophyll	a green pigment found in plants that helps them absorb light and produce their food
conifers	trees and shrubs that have cones and are mostly evergreen
deciduous	trees that shed their leaves during a season of the year
dehydration	when something is dry, after water loss
endangered	at risk of extinction
estimate	an approximate calculation
evergreen	a plant that has leaves which remain green year-round
evolved	when something has developed over a long period of time
extinct	having no living members; a species that has died out
fossil fuel	fuel made up of the remains of organisms that have been compressed underground
frond	a large leaf, like those on a fern, that splits into different sections
germination	the process whereby something begins to grow and develop, such as a seedling sprouting out from a seed
grafting	attaching one part of a plant to another plant to grow together
habitat	the environment or home of a creature or plant
herbivore	the description of an organism that eats only plants
invasive species	organisms that invade and modify an environment of which they are not naturally a part
liverwort	a small green nonflowering plant, similar to moss but with a more distinctive leaf structure
moss	a green, dense, nonflowering plant that grows in damp areas
nectar	a sugary substance produced by plants and made into honey by bees
nutrients	a substance that is beneficial to growth and well-being
organism	a living thing
oxygen	a gas that plants produce and humans breathe in to live
parasite	an organism that lives off another organism
photosynthesis	the process by which plants create their own food and produce oxygen
pollen	dustlike grains on a flower that are carried to another plant for fertilization
pollination	the process whereby pollen is transferred from one plant to another
rhizome	an underground rootlike structure that bears shoots
sap	a fluid that circulates around a plant, carrying nutrients and water
species	living things that contain shared characteristics, e.g. human beings
spores	the reproductive cells of ferns and mosses
stamen	the fertilizing organ of a plant
toxic	a poisonous substance

INDEX